CREAT

WITH
Helen Squire

Hand & Machine Quilting

For Nola —
May you quiet
in Peace
Helen Squire
Paducah KY
1999

American Quilter's Society
P.O. Box 3290 • Paducah, KY 42002-3290

D0826045

Located in Paducah, Kentucky, the American Quilter's Society (AQS) is dedicated to promoting the accomplishments of today's quilters. Through its publications and events, AQS strives to honor today's quiltmakers and their work and to inspire future creativity and innovation in quiltmaking.

COPY EDITOR: BARBARA SMITH
TECHNICAL EDITOR: HELEN SQUIRE
BOOK DESIGN/ILLUSTRATIONS: MICHAEL BUCKINGHAM
COVER DESIGN: MICHAEL BUCKINGHAM
PHOTOGRAPHY: CHARLES R. LYNCH

Library of Congress Cataloging-in-Publication Data

Squire, Helen.
        Create with Helen Squire : hand & machine quilting.
                        p.   cm.
        ISBN 1-57432-724-0
            1. Quilting--Patterns.   2. Machine quilting--Patterns.
    I. American Quilter's Society.   II. Title.
    TT835.S657   1999
    746.46'041--dc21   99-47336
                                                          CIP

Additional copies of this book may be ordered from the American Quilter's Society, PO Box 3290, Paducah, KY 42002-3290 @ $18.95. Add $2.00 for postage and handling.

Printed in the U.S.A. by Image Graphics, Paducah, KY

Contents

Dedication

I have been blessed with the opportunity of having five quilting design books published by the American Quilter's Society. My patterns are named upon creation in honor of my family, friends, students, or the places where inspiration struck. There are over 410 patterns combined in the series, and I have yet to run out of names or ideas.

This book is dedicated to four special people in my life —

Laura and Brian, Susan, and Vanessa.

God bless them.

Introduction

I have written magazine columns called *Dear Helen, Can You Tell Me?* and *Helen's Hints* for a good many years. As my visage has aged, so my quilting philosophy has matured.

As the question and answer expert for *Lady's Circle Patchwork Quilts* for 20 years, and the designer of *Creative Quilting Designs* in the *American Quilter* magazine in recent years, I have come to realize that it was necessary to adapt my traditional quilting beliefs. They needed to be changed to better accommodate today's hand and machine quilters, people with busy, time-evaporating lifestyles who need faster, easier, more successful ways to mark and quilt their projects. And, I had to learn how to do this without sacrificing the principles of good design and the timeless appeal of the finished quilt.

There is one quilting question that is universal. *"How do you mark your quilt?"** I have always answered, "It's not *how* you mark, it's *what* you mark."

Ask yourself: How much quilting is structurally needed? Is the pattern large enough to fill the space or area to be quilted? Are you marking before or after the batting has been added? Is there a theme to the quilt? A mood? Does it require flowing curves or straight lines to compliment the fabric or patchwork? Are you quilting by hand or with a sewing or quilting machine? These are the types of questions that need to be considered *before* you start marking the quilt!

My response to *"How do you plan the quilting?"* is so involved that it could easily fill a book. A book exactly like this one.

*I use combinations of chalk pencils in assorted colors, water erasable pens, rulers, cutout plastic stencils, silhouette cardboard, and an underneath light source for copying my pre-planned quilting design from a muslin master (see page 35).

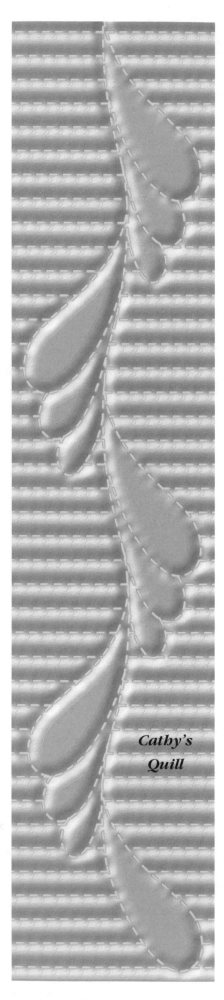

Cathy's Quill

Checklist *of* Quilting Possibilities

Designing is taking the materials you have at hand and improving on their arrangement. Whether it be arranging flowers from the garden, hanging pictures on a wall, or planning a wardrobe – we are all designers. *To select a quilting pattern* for an individual quilt, you need to train yourself to look for a winning combination, by trying a variety of placement possibilities, then discarding what does not work. When this process becomes automatic, you will have a way to create designs *that custom fit your every need!*

☐ **Adapt**
To fit an original purpose with partial changes.

☐ **Adjust**
To shift a determined order for better alignment.

☐ **Arrange**
To put in a different order.

☐ **Copy**
A reproduction of a pattern.

☐ **Continuous**
Connected or extended without a break.

☐ **Connect**
To combine, close, complete patterns.

☐ **Combine**
To unite two or more drawings to make a new pattern.

☐ **Design**
To plan and make with art or skill.

☐ **Draft**
To use precise tools to draw an accurate pattern.

☐ **Draw**
To sketch or diagram an idea.

☐ **Duplicate**
A double likeness.

☐ **Element**
A simple part of any pattern.

☐ **Emphasize**
To make prominent or distinct.

☐ **Enlarge**
To increase the size, widen.

☐ **Face**
To turn in a given direction.

☐ **Flop**
Varied reduplication of the pattern; to move it up and down, over the top or bottom.

☐ **Lengthen**
To make longer, *not* wider.

☐ **Minimize** *(backgrounds)*
To reduce to the smallest possible amount.

☐ **Mirror Image**
A perfect opposite reflection.

☐ **Miter**
The junction of patterns at an equally divided angle, usually in a corner.

☐ **Modify**
To make changes that slightly alter the shape.

☐ **Nestle**
To place patterns close together.

☐ **Offset**
To stagger the rows.

☐ **Omit**
To choose *not* to include certain parts of the pattern.

☐ **Pivot**
To swing or rotate on a point.

☐ **Place**
To put in a particular position.

☐ **Photocopy**
A reproduction method used to make extra copies and change sizes.

☐ **Recognize**
To realize the motif, or element of the design.

☐ **Reduce**
To make smaller in size.

☐ **Repeats**
To use one figure in frequent order.

☐ **Reposition**
To place in a different position.

☐ **Reverse**
To move or turn in the opposite direction.

☐ **Rotate**
To turn on its axis.

☐ **Set on Point**
To put a pattern or design in a diamond-like position.

☐ **Set Square**
To put a pattern or design in a squared-off position.

☐ **Shorten**
To lessen selected parts.

☐ **Simplify**
To make less complex.

☐ **Stretch**
To elongate, exaggerate, or spread to a new size or shape.

☐ **Trace**
To copy a pattern on a superimposed transparent sheet or to draw around cut-out shapes.

☐ **Width**
Measurement of a quilt pattern taken from side to side, *or* top to bottom.

Terminology *Explained*

Combine the best of both worlds! Incorporate both hand and machine quilting techniques to finish your projects sooner. Spend your energy and your time where it counts! Use hand quilting for design details and machine quilting for structural support and allover quilting.

bold fabric – fancy quilting won't show here

plain blocks are perfect for hand quilted feathered wreaths

inner border is quilted in-the-ditch for support

extra stitches needed here to prevent long strips from sagging

outer border is free-flowing machine quilted

binding is sewn by machine

quarter corner blocks use ¼ of quilt pattern

half blocks on sides use ½ of quilt pattern

full blocks are set on point

foundation pieced patchwork blocks quilted in the seams

½" outline quilted (off the seams) inside plain blocks by machine

each block is machine quilted in-the-ditch

Pink Baskets by Helen Johnson, Brookfield, Vermont

❏ STRUCTURAL QUILTING
The need to use enough quilting to hold the batting in place during regular wear and cleaning. Open areas vary – polyester can be quilted every 4" to 6", but cotton needs to be quilted every 1" to 3".

❏ IN-THE-DITCH QUILTING
Quilting the side without the extra seam allowance. Usually fabrics have been pressed to darker colors which have been pre-selected to create recognizable shapes; i.e. baskets, stars, etc.

❏ OUTLINE QUILTING
This is done to emphasize a shape. (1) For *patchwork,* quilting is used ¼" away from the seams, and (2) for *appliqué,* quilting is done as close to the sewn shape (apple, heart, flower) as possible, or (3) for *combinations,* outline quilting is done next to a shape, and another row of quilting is added ¼" to ½" away. Multiply rows of outline stitches are called echo, contour, or ripple quilting.

❏ DESIGN QUILTING
The best part! The *whip cream* areas are wide-open places where no seams impede the stitches. Your finest quilting design, pattern, and/or nicest stitches should be used here. *Examples:* Double Wedding Rings, Irish Chains, and all whitework quilts.

- The sawtooth inner border is outline quilted off the seams and in-the-ditch.

- The large grid gives movement and repetition to the points.

- The Flying Geese blocks are quilted in-the-ditch and with straight rows.

- Machine stippled backgrounds surround each hand-quilted flower design from the first *Dear Helen* book.

- The leaves, birds, berries, and flowers are outline quilted, with extra details added.

- Wide outer border and binding are machined stitched.

Helen Johnson and I have successfully team-taught a workshop we called The Best of Both Worlds *at the Vermont Quilt Festival and the AQS Quilt Show. Workshop participants learn the technical methods necessary to quilt on the sewing machine and the design processes needed for a good-looking layout. It's the combination of less-time techniques with time-less traditions that quilters seem to want, going into the twenty-first century.*

- Blocks were set square on a full fabric piece which eliminated bulky seams to quilt over.

- Helen Johnson sandwiched just the center top over the batting as a faster method for quilting the straight grid lines.

- Next, she *appli-quilted* the hearts and flowers with a decorative hem stitch through all three layers.

- The inner and outer borders were then machine sewn in place over the batting to cover the ends of the grid. (Similar to strip or lap quilting.)

- Parallel lines of quilting were done across the border fabric *before* the swags, hearts, and corner bows were again stitched through the layers in her special *appli-quilt* technique.

Geese in Flight by Helen Johnson

Hearts and Flowers by Helen Johnson

Victorian Valentine

PULL-OUT PATTERN 11" BLOCK

Chapter One

Soft Curves

☐ Make four copies of *Victorian Valentine.*

☐ Rotate and connect repeats as shown in illustration at right.

☐ Set pattern square.

☐ Use four repeats above for a 12" quilted block, or use the 11" pattern in the pull-out pattern sheet.

☐ Enlarge pattern to fit the area to be quilted.

Placement Diagram: Intricate quilting an be used when it really counts for wholecloth, whitework, and tone-on-tone quilts.

☐ Place four blocks together, just touching, as shown above.

☐ Determine the amount of open area left unquilted. (Shaded here to illustrate negative space.)

☐ Add background grids to flatten the fabric if there is too much open space, such as

    ☐ Cross-hatching   ☐ Stippling

    ☐ Diagonal lines   ☐ Hanging Diamonds

See Chapter 5 for actual-size, geometric-grid patterns.

Helen's Hint:
This is also what the back of the quilt would look like after quilting *Victorian Valentine.*

Victorian Nosegay

To create a nice, large-scale quilting pattern suitable for a medallion quilt:

☐ Make extra copies of the connected designs *Victorian Valentine* (four repeats) or *Viola Remembered* (eight repeats).

☐ Use a light source underneath the copies to see the design developing.

☐ Place one complete set on top of another set. Tape bottom layer in place to hold.

☐ Rotate the top paper copy until the patterns overlap, creating the design shown above.

☐ Simplify the design by omitting duplicated details while keeping the essence of the original.

☐ Redraft one-fourth or one-eighth of the design with smooth, flowing lines.

☐ Enlarge to fit the area to be quilted.

☐ Rename the pattern. I call this entirely new quilting design *Victorian Nosegay*.

- Make eight copies: four facing left, four facing right (reversed).

- Join patterns to create heart shape (✱) as shown in illustration.

- Place pattern on point.

- Enlarge or reduce to fit the area to be quilted.

Placement Diagram:
Design can also be used for wholecloth quilting.

Adapted from the pattern *Viola's Vine*, as seen in the book *Dear Helen, Can You Tell Me...All About Quilting Designs?* (AQS 1987).

Viola Remembered

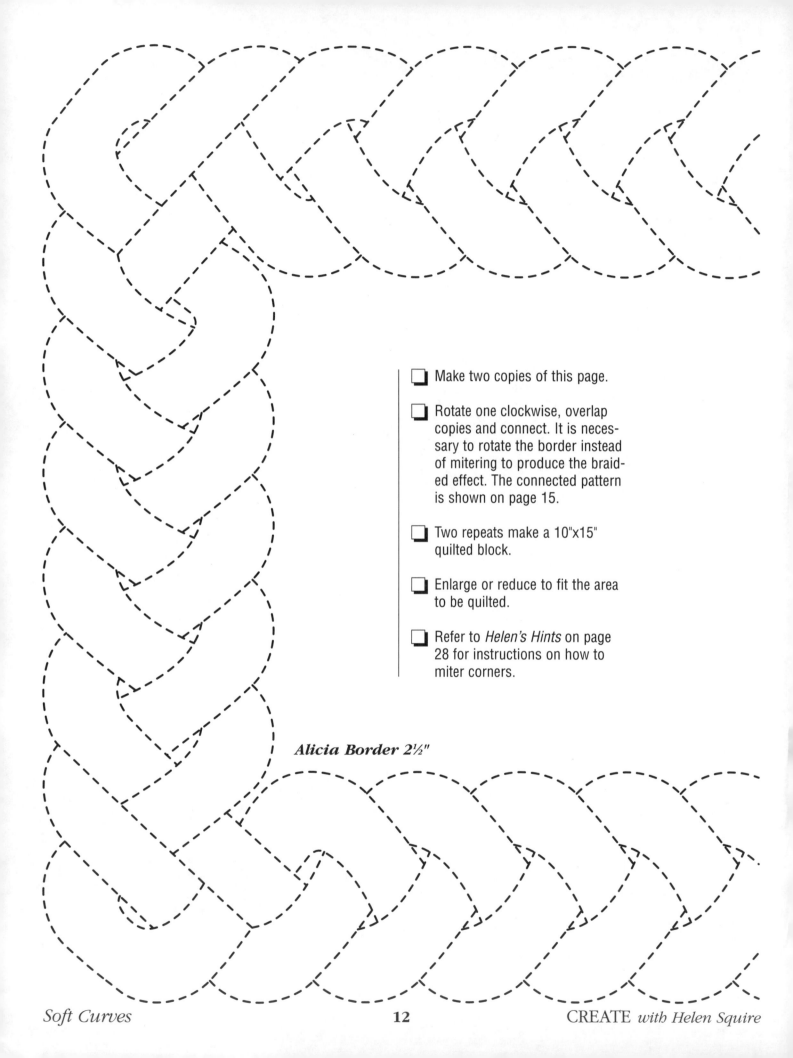

■ Make two copies of this page.

■ Rotate one clockwise, overlap copies and connect. It is necessary to rotate the border instead of mitering to produce the braided effect. The connected pattern is shown on page 15.

■ Two repeats make a 10"x15" quilted block.

■ Enlarge or reduce to fit the area to be quilted.

■ Refer to *Helen's Hints* on page 28 for instructions on how to miter corners.

Alicia Border 2½"

Alicia 1½"

Alicia 5"

Alicia 3"

Alicia 4"

Adapted from the pattern *Alicia's Braid*, as seen in the book, *...ask Helen, All About Quilting Designs* (AQS 1990).

Braided Corners

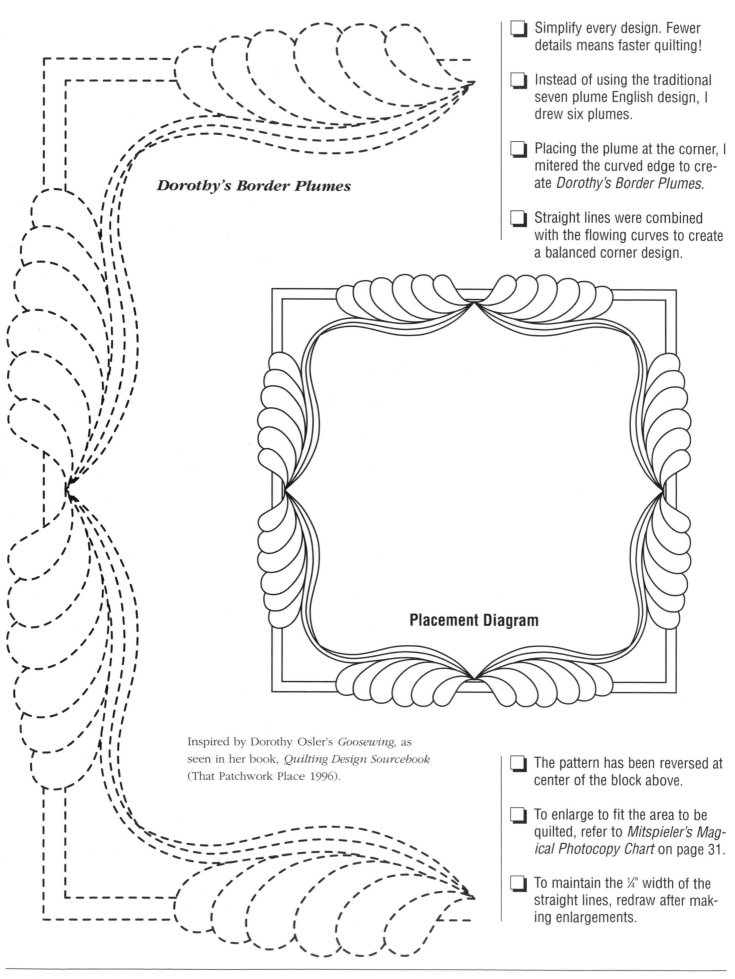

Dorothy's Border Plumes

- Simplify every design. Fewer details means faster quilting!

- Instead of using the traditional seven plume English design, I drew six plumes.

- Placing the plume at the corner, I mitered the curved edge to create *Dorothy's Border Plumes*.

- Straight lines were combined with the flowing curves to create a balanced corner design.

Placement Diagram

Inspired by Dorothy Osler's *Goosewing*, as seen in her book, *Quilting Design Sourcebook* (That Patchwork Place 1996).

- The pattern has been reversed at center of the block above.

- To enlarge to fit the area to be quilted, refer to *Mitspieler's Magical Photocopy Chart* on page 31.

- To maintain the ¼" width of the straight lines, redraw after making enlargements.

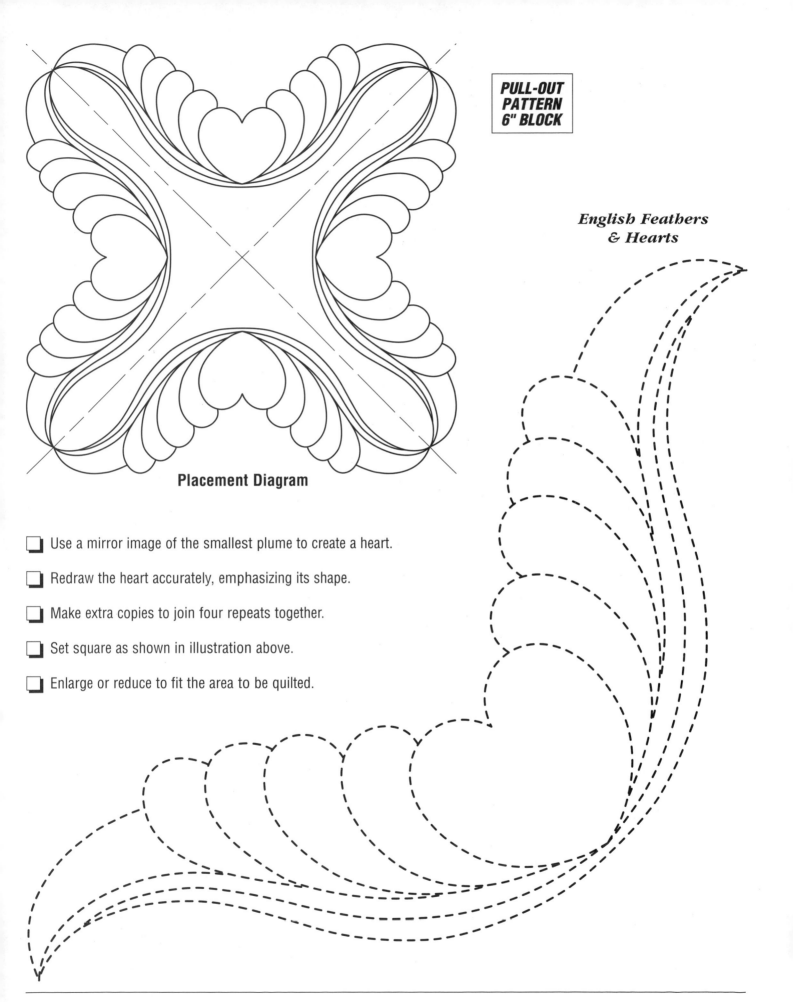

*English Feathers
& Hearts*

Placement Diagram

☐ Use a mirror image of the smallest plume to create a heart.

☐ Redraw the heart accurately, emphasizing its shape.

☐ Make extra copies to join four repeats together.

☐ Set square as shown in illustration above.

☐ Enlarge or reduce to fit the area to be quilted.

Place with design facing outward (above).

Place with design facing toward center (below).

Enlarge to fit the area to be quilted.

Placement Diagrams

Annette's Machine Curves

**Annette's
Bavarian Scrolls**

Placement Diagram

☐ Combine both versions by enlarging proportionately to fit one within the other.

☐ Add a background grid to flatten open area. *See page 63.*

As seen in *American Quilter* magazine, Spring 1998, and *Dear Helen, Can You Tell Me?* (AQS 1987).

Helen's Hints:
Start a collection of oblong quilting designs. They are hard to find yet very helpful, since the average quilt is made to fit a bed, which has rectangular measurements.

Placement Diagram

☐ Make copies: two left views, two right views (reversed) to create a picture frame effect.

☐ Place copies just touching along sides, as shown above.

☐ Enlarge pattern to fit the area to be quilted.

☐ Add quilting, appliqué, or patchwork to enlargements as the open area becomes bigger.

☐ This design can be combined with *Annette's Bavarian Scrolls* on page 21.

Annette's Corner

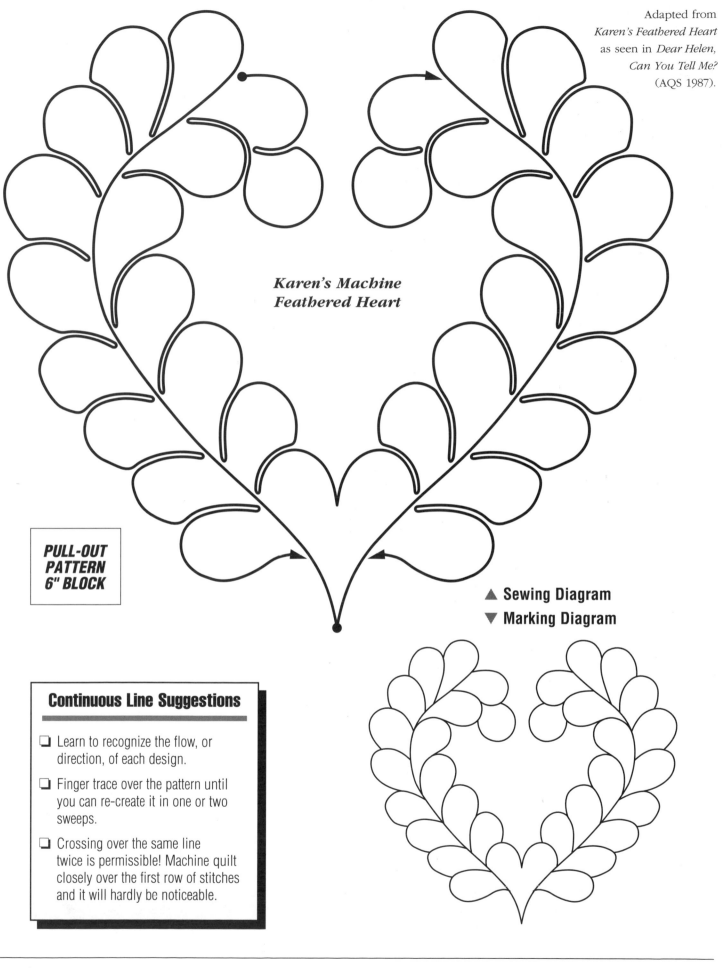

Adapted from
Karen's Feathered Heart
as seen in *Dear Helen,
Can You Tell Me?*
(AQS 1987).

*Karen's Machine
Feathered Heart*

PULL-OUT
PATTERN
6" BLOCK

▲ Sewing Diagram
▼ Marking Diagram

Continuous Line Suggestions

❏ Learn to recognize the flow, or direction, of each design.

❏ Finger trace over the pattern until you can re-create it in one or two sweeps.

❏ Crossing over the same line twice is permissible! Machine quilt closely over the first row of stitches and it will hardly be noticeable.

Chapter Two

Strong Lineals

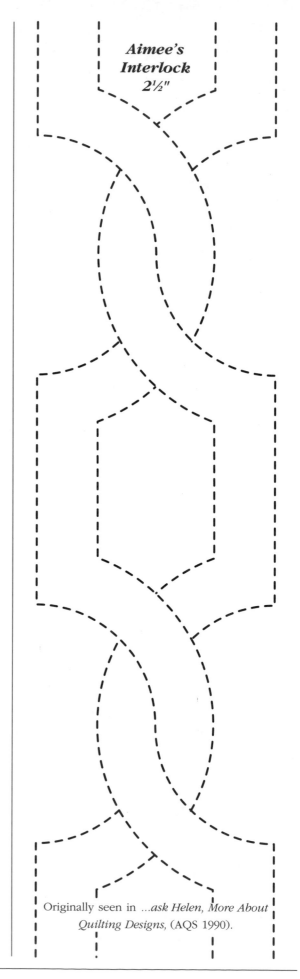

Aimee's Interlock 2½"

- ☐ Adapt this pattern to fit the exact size of your quilt.

- ☐ Enlarge *Aimee's Interlock* to fit the **width** you need.

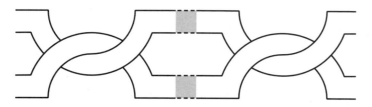

- ☐ Cut and add spacers to **lengthen** and extend the sides of the border.

- ☐ Omit the straight lines connecting the interlocking curves to **shorten** the pattern.

- ☐ Try not to adjust the fancy detail, because it is the essence of the design and the most difficult area to fix.

- ☐ Redraw the new shapes. Make extra copies to plan the repeats. Do not reverse or interlocking effect will be lost.

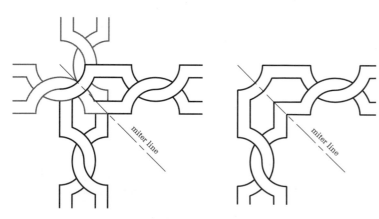

- ☐ Plan the pattern up to a diagonal line, stop, rotate, and continue to trace the pattern, to turn the corners as shown in the illustrations (above).

- ☐ Add straight box-like outer lines to minimize the background areas in *Merdie's Maze*. These lines would be quilted in-the-ditch, along the border of a pieced quilt.

Originally seen in ...*ask Helen, More About Quilting Designs,* (AQS 1990).

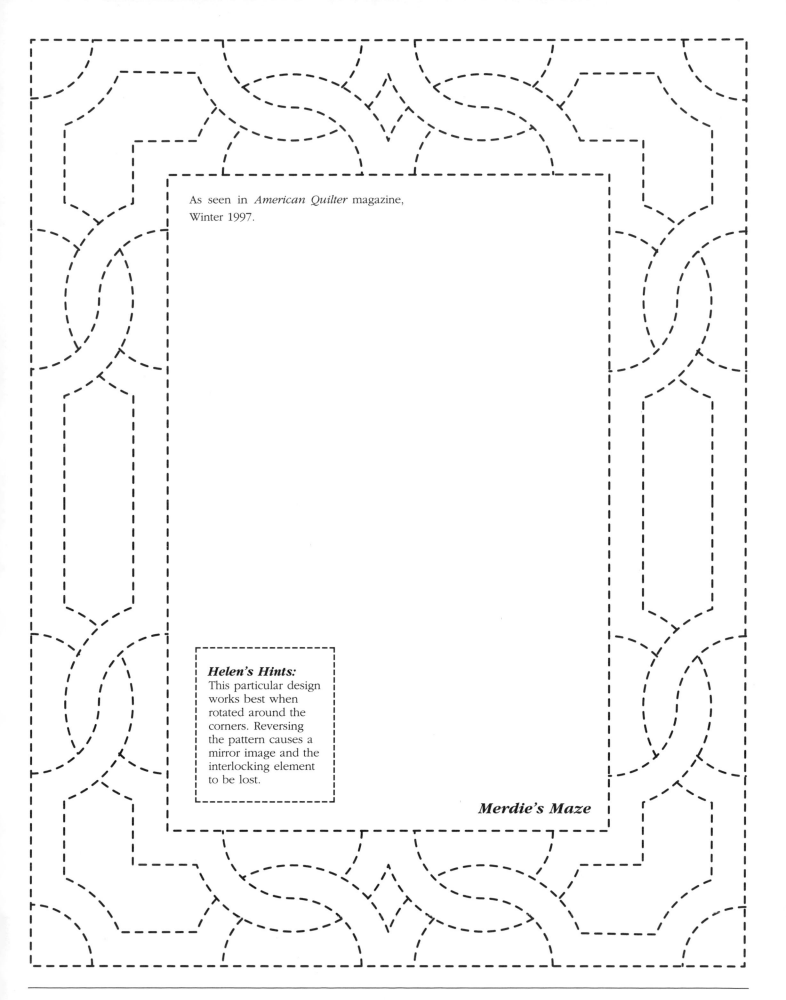

As seen in *American Quilter* magazine, Winter 1997.

Helen's Hints:
This particular design works best when rotated around the corners. Reversing the pattern causes a mirror image and the interlocking element to be lost.

Merdie's Maze

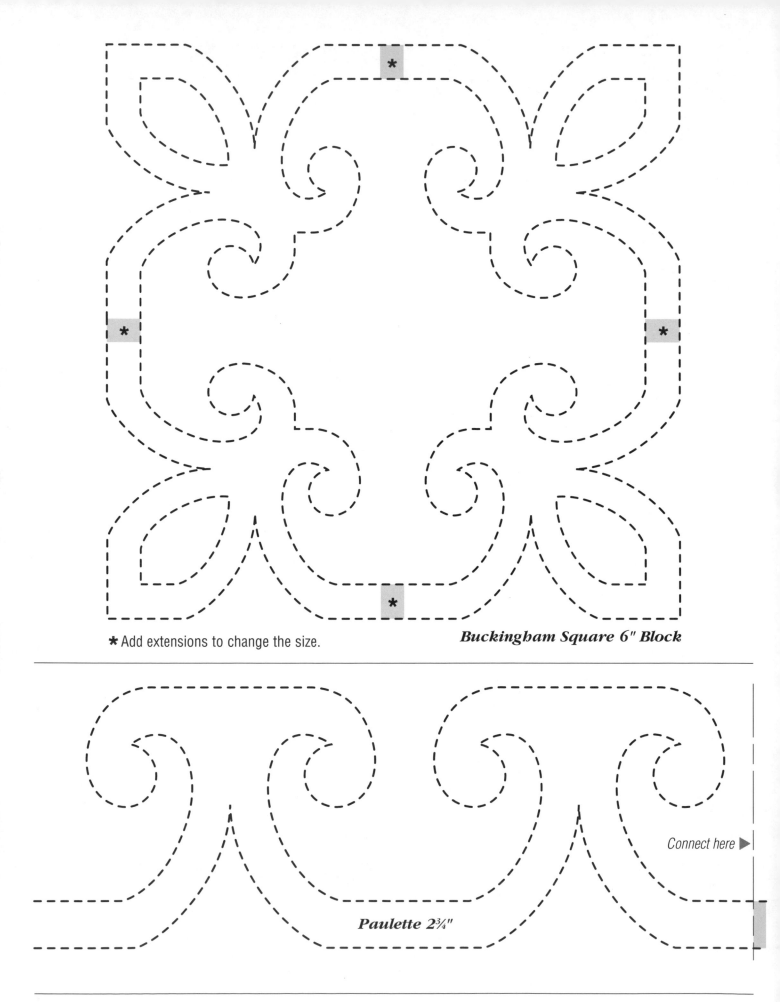

✱ Add extensions to change the size.

Buckingham Square 6" Block

Connect here ▶

Paulette 2¾"

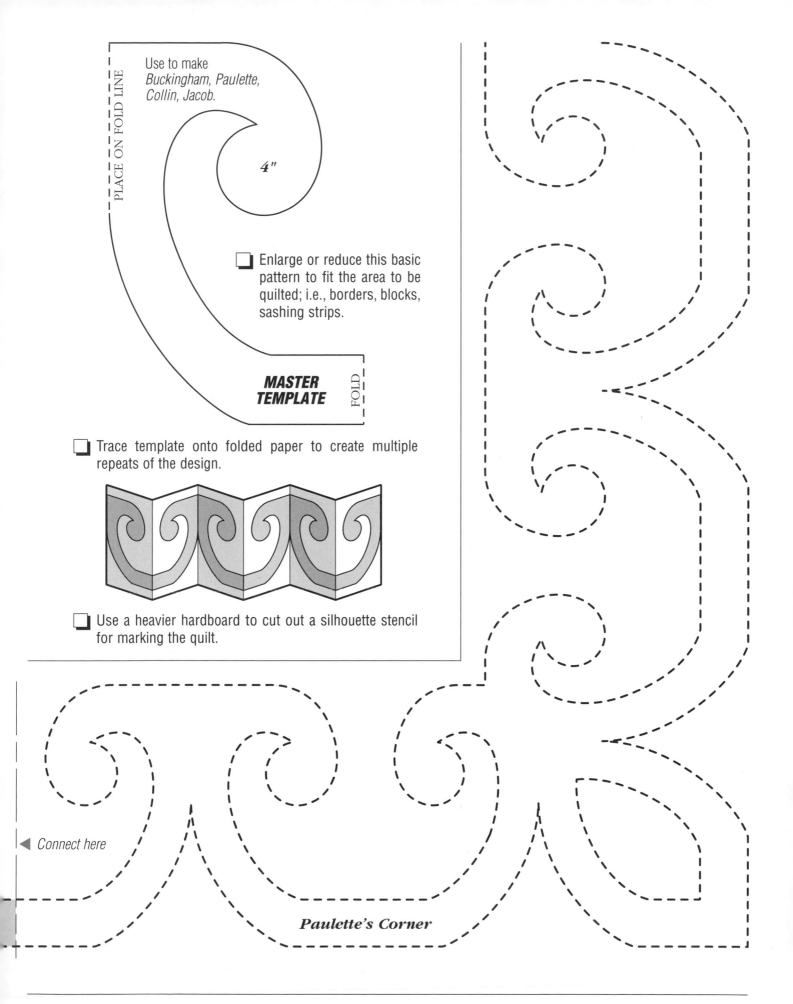

PLACE ON FOLD LINE

Use to make
*Buckingham, Paulette,
Collin, Jacob.*

4"

☐ Enlarge or reduce this basic pattern to fit the area to be quilted; i.e., borders, blocks, sashing strips.

MASTER TEMPLATE

FOLD

☐ Trace template onto folded paper to create multiple repeats of the design.

☐ Use a heavier hardboard to cut out a silhouette stencil for marking the quilt.

◄ *Connect here*

Paulette's Corner

Collin 3"

PULL-OUT PATTERN 6" BORDER

Left down

right

left

Left up

left

right

Helen's Hint:

Any pattern can be made to turn a corner perfectly in four different ways: left down, left up, right down, and right up, as long as you make extra copies, one of which is reversed. All of these versions use the same basic pattern, Paulette (page 26).

Notice how different the quilting designs look on these two pages. Collin is a delicate rounded shape; Jacob is a strong geometric column. Both have been mitered at the corner and their mirror images can be repeated around the quilt.

Jacob 3"

Right down

left

right

Right up

right

left

**PULL-OUT
PATTERN
5" BORDER**

☐ Use two copies of *Paulette*. (Master template is already reversed.)

☐ Align and staple copies right side together at either end.

☐ Fold back paper to reveal pleasing patterns. Crease each new design on the diagonal as it unfolds.

☐ Try all four versions. Refer to the illustrations above.

☐ Select one or two favorites and redraft accurately. Make extra copies and determine the size and amount of repeats needed.

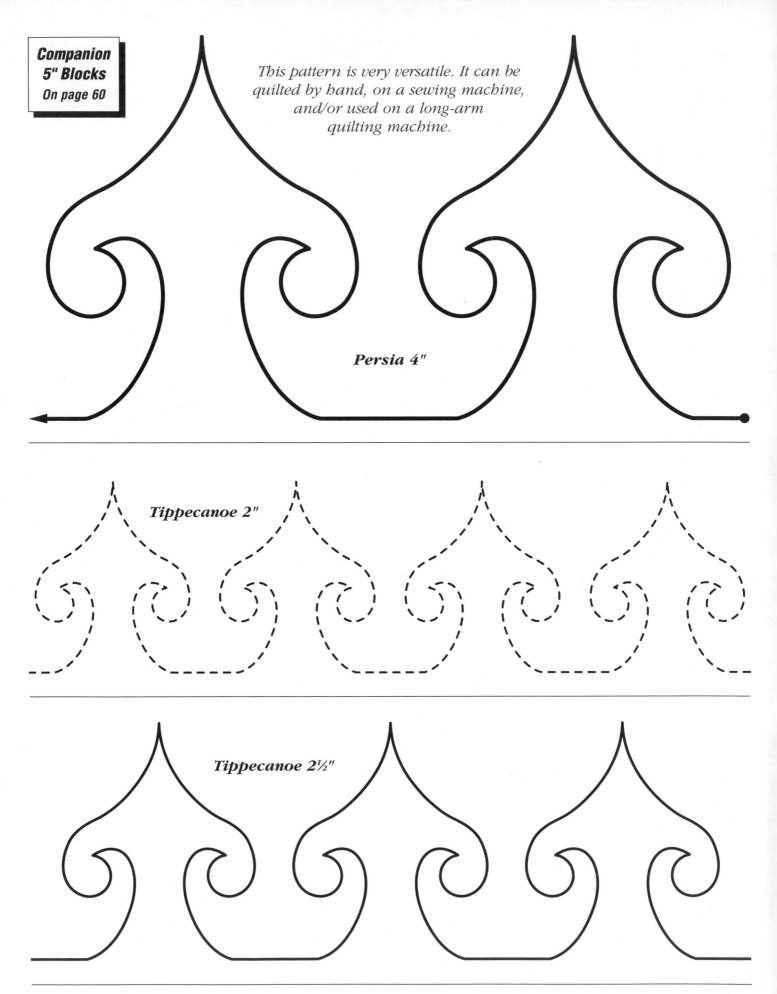

This pattern is very versatile. It can be quilted by hand, on a sewing machine, and/or used on a long-arm quilting machine.

Persia 4"

Tippecanoe 2"

Tippecanoe 2½"

To enlarge 4" to 7", find 4" in the left column and look across the top to find 7". The percentage is 175%. To reduce 4" to 3", find 4" and look across to 3". The reduction is 75% of the original.

ENLARGING & REDUCING Photocopying Chart

	3"	4"	5"	6"	7"	8"	9"	10"
3"	100%	133%	166%	200%	233%	266%	300%	333%
4"	75%	100%	125%	150%	175%	200%	225%	250%
5"	60%	80%	100%	120%	140%	160%	180%	200%
6"	50%	67%	83%	100%	117%	133%	150%	167%
7"	43%	52%	71%	86%	100%	114%	128%	143%
8"	37%	50%	62%	75%	87%	100%	112%	125%
9"	33%	44%	55%	66%	77%	88%	100%	111%
10"	30%	40%	50%	60%	70%	80%	90%	100%
11"	27%	36%	45%	54%	63%	72%	81%	90%
12"	25%	34%	42%	50%	59%	67%	76%	84%

Persian Corner

Adapted from *Mitspieler's Photocopy Chart*, as seen in *Show Me Helen, How to Use Quilting Designs* (AQS 1993).

☐ Use two repeats of *Paulette* (page 26), setting the first one on top of the second row. Omit the straight line between rows (✱) to form a new shape. I call this new design *Persia.*

☐ Reduce or enlarge the **width,** the height of the row(s), to fit the area to be quilted.

☐ Copy and connect enough repeats to form the **length** required for the quilt.

☐ Follow suggested mitered design as shown here for corners.

Machine Quilting Diagram

☐ Mark and quilt in a continuous line.

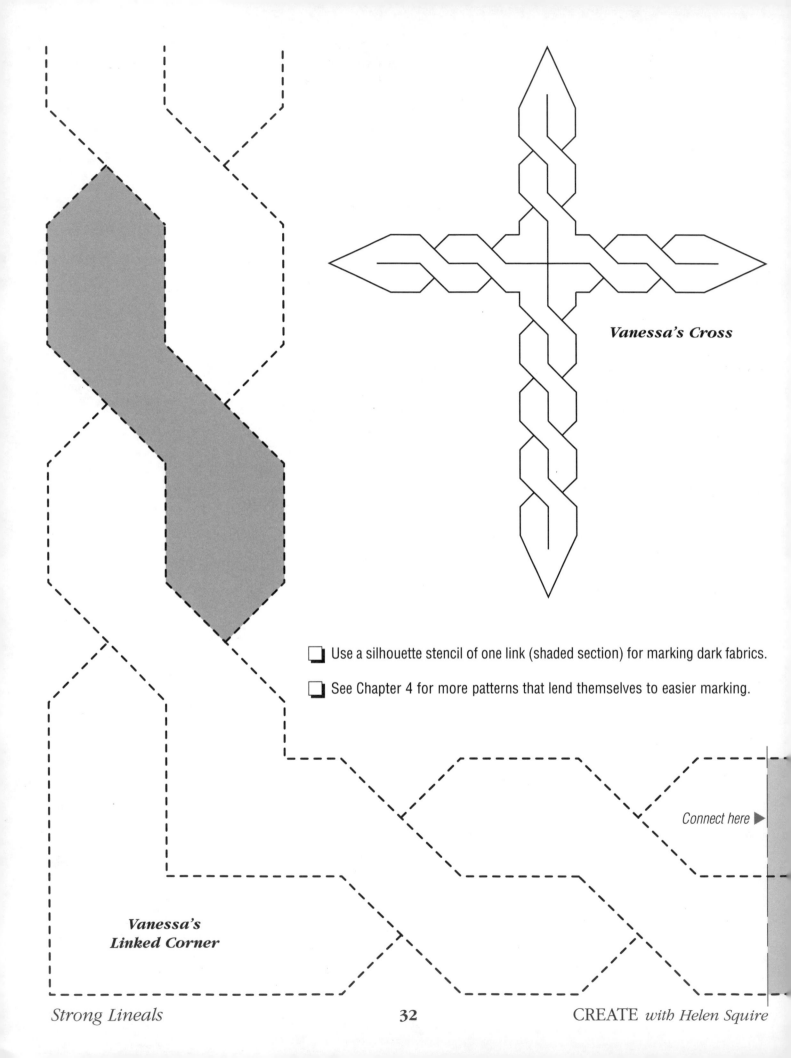

Vanessa's Cross

☐ Use a silhouette stencil of one link (shaded section) for marking dark fabrics.

☐ See Chapter 4 for more patterns that lend themselves to easier marking.

Connect here ▶

*Vanessa's
Linked Corner*

How to Select the Proper Quilting Design

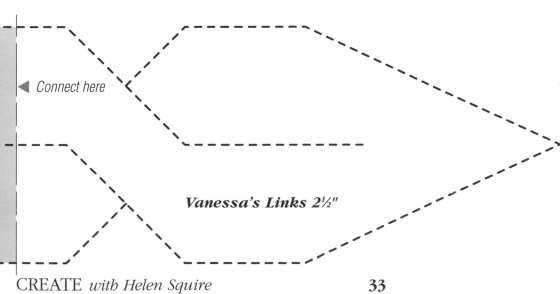

Dining Car Derailed by Jan Berkley, Arlington Heights, Illinois.

☐ **Consider the pattern:** Geometric patchwork usually calls for flowing lines for movement.

☐ **Consider the fabric:** Jan Berkley's blue and white fabric already includes a good swirling navy print, yet its elaborate design prohibits any fancy quilting.

☐ **Emphasize the design:** Choosing *Vanessa's Link* reinforces the straight angular look of the quilt.

☐ **Quilting-in-the-ditch:** Structurally holds the blocks together.

☐ **Combine and measure:** Jan's double border (9") forms a larger quilting space.

☐ **Consider the size:** Enlarge or reduce the pattern to fit that area.

◄ *Connect here*

Vanessa's Links 2½"

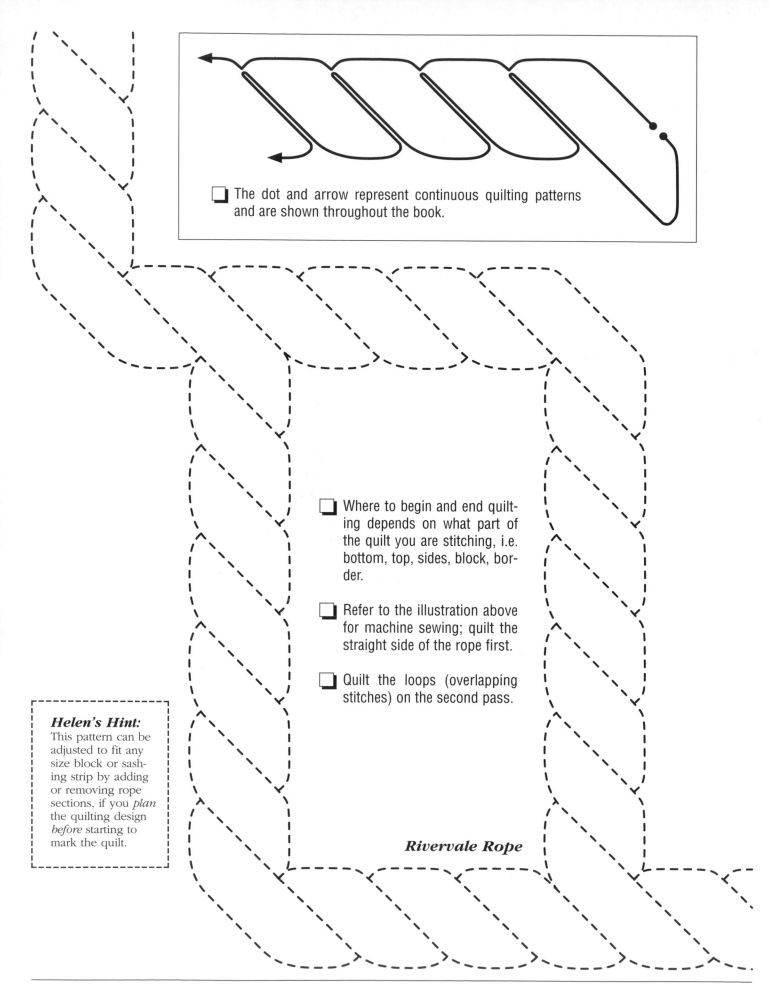

The dot and arrow represent continuous quilting patterns and are shown throughout the book.

Where to begin and end quilting depends on what part of the quilt you are stitching, i.e. bottom, top, sides, block, border.

Refer to the illustration above for machine sewing; quilt the straight side of the rope first.

Quilt the loops (overlapping stitches) on the second pass.

Helen's Hint:
This pattern can be adjusted to fit any size block or sashing strip by adding or removing rope sections, if you *plan* the quilting design *before* starting to mark the quilt.

Rivervale Rope

Tips for Making a Muslin Master of the Quilting Design Layout

- Instead of sheets of paper, create a master pattern *drawn on muslin.* It's durable, easy to fold, does not rip, and is cheaper than large-sized paper!

- Design and plan for one-quarter of the layout plus a two-inch overlap which allows you to see if the pattern is to be flipped, flopped, rotated, mitered at corners, or reversed at the center of the quilt, etc.

- Use photocopies as often as necessary to plan the repeats but mark the muslin using the original pattern for accuracy. Patterns can be stretched or distorted while being photocopied.

- For background grids, start a reference collection. Invest the time to draft straight lines, hanging diamonds, and crosshatching grids in a variety of sizes on a muslin master. Simply slip them under the fabric to be marked, position as desired, and trace them carefully on the quilt top with a long ruler. Save the grid to be used again and again.

- Draw the quilting design *on the muslin* with a fine-line indelible black marker. Light-colored quilt tops are pinned on top of the muslin, and the entire design traced with a regular color-matched chalk pencil.

- Refer to the pattern layout when you mark the actual quilt. Use a light box, sliding glass door, glass coffee table, etc., for backlighting. Tape the muslin in place before marking to prevent shifting.

- I recommend the following marking tools: chalk pencils in assorted colors, pre-tested water-erasable pens, masking tape in assorted widths, True-Angle Ruler™ and other long rulers.

- Use a *silhouette stencil* for marking after layering or on dark fabric. A shape is easier to trace around if it's cut from heavy cardboard, manila folders, or plastic. Follow the muslin layout whenever you mark.

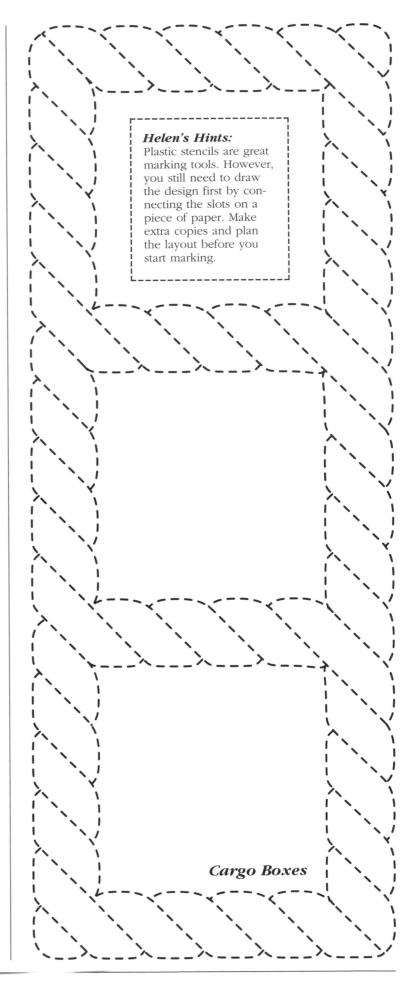

Helen's Hints:
Plastic stencils are great marking tools. However, you still need to draw the design first by connecting the slots on a piece of paper. Make extra copies and plan the layout before you start marking.

Cargo Boxes

Chapter Three

Flowing Florals

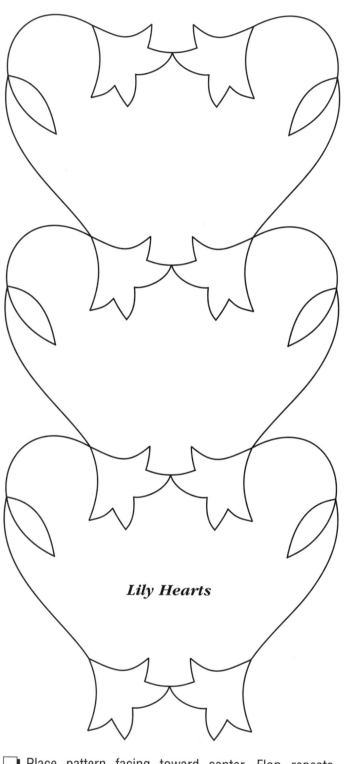

Lily Hearts

Lily Shields

☐ Place pattern facing toward center. Flop repeats, touching flowers to form a scalloped heart-like shape.

☐ Place pattern with design facing outward. Flop repeats and position as shown above, creating *Lily Shields*.

This pattern is a very good teaching tool. I've used it before in *Dear Helen* (AQS 1987), *Helen's Guide* (AQS 1996), and *Helen's Hints* (Summer 1998).

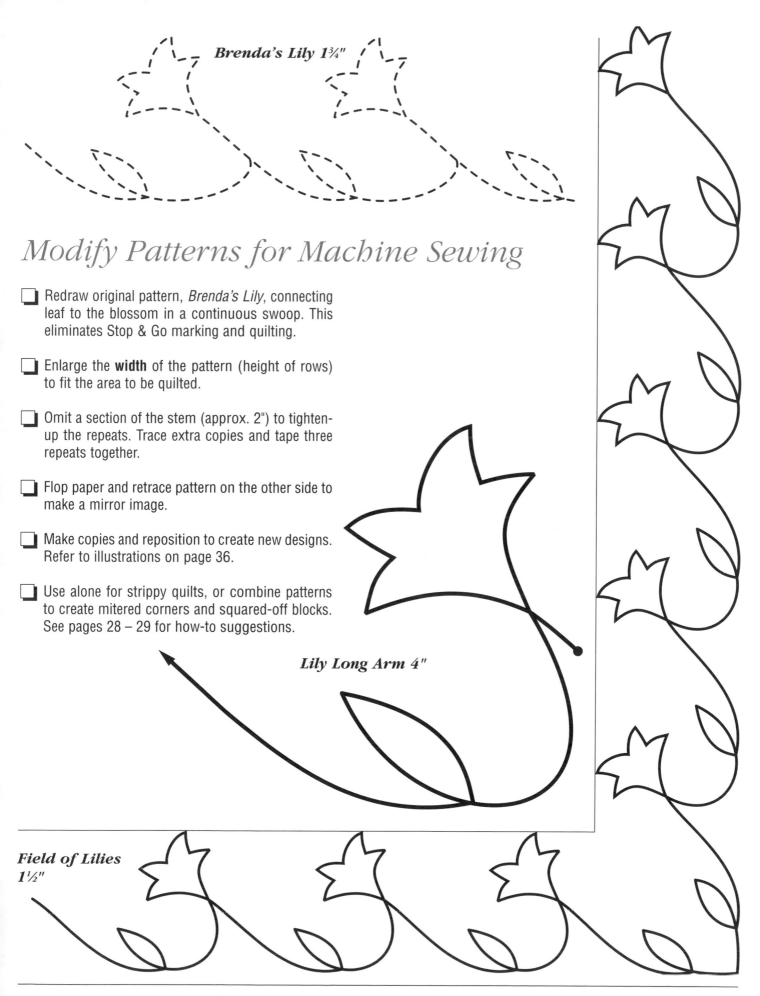

Brenda's Lily 1¾"

Modify Patterns for Machine Sewing

☐ Redraw original pattern, *Brenda's Lily*, connecting leaf to the blossom in a continuous swoop. This eliminates Stop & Go marking and quilting.

☐ Enlarge the **width** of the pattern (height of rows) to fit the area to be quilted.

☐ Omit a section of the stem (approx. 2") to tighten-up the repeats. Trace extra copies and tape three repeats together.

☐ Flop paper and retrace pattern on the other side to make a mirror image.

☐ Make copies and reposition to create new designs. Refer to illustrations on page 36.

☐ Use alone for strippy quilts, or combine patterns to create mitered corners and squared-off blocks. See pages 28 – 29 for how-to suggestions.

Lily Long Arm 4"

Field of Lilies 1½"

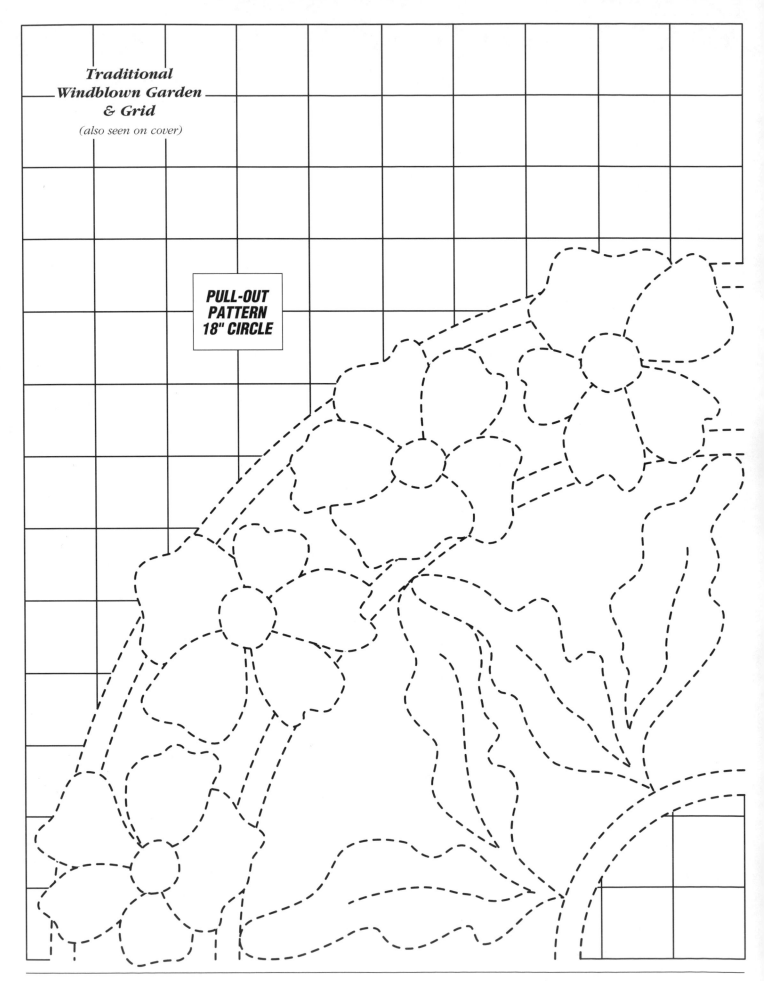

Traditional Windblown Garden & Grid

(also seen on cover)

PULL-OUT
PATTERN
18" CIRCLE

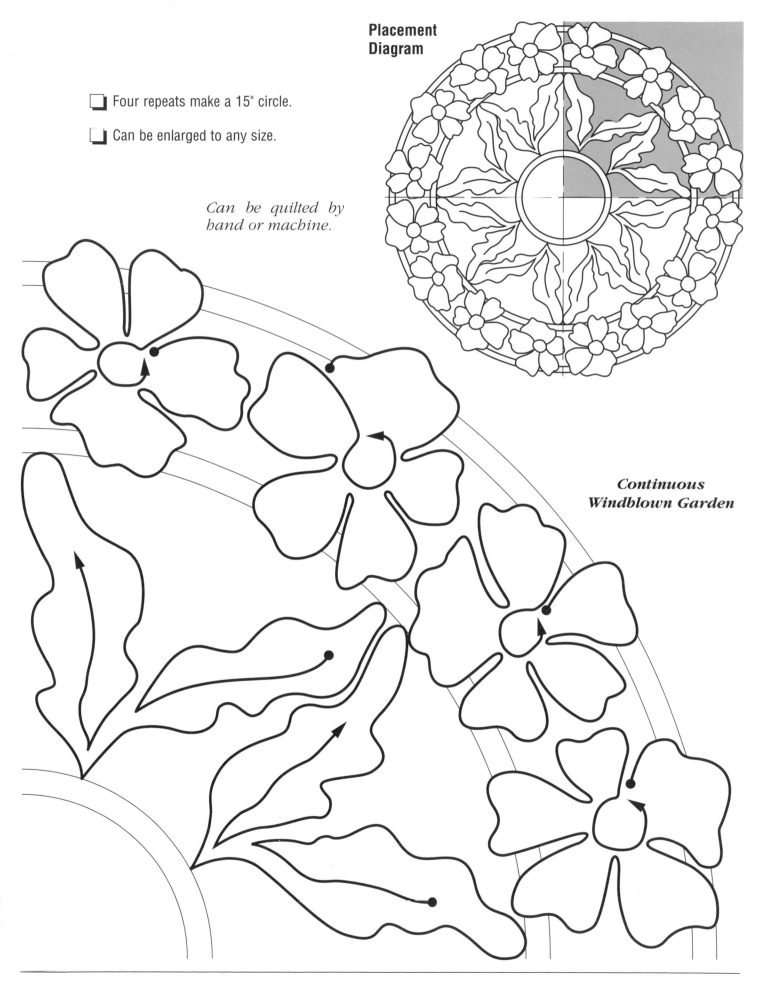

Placement Diagram

☐ Four repeats make a 15" circle.

☐ Can be enlarged to any size.

Can be quilted by hand or machine.

Continuous Windblown Garden

Windblown Flowers

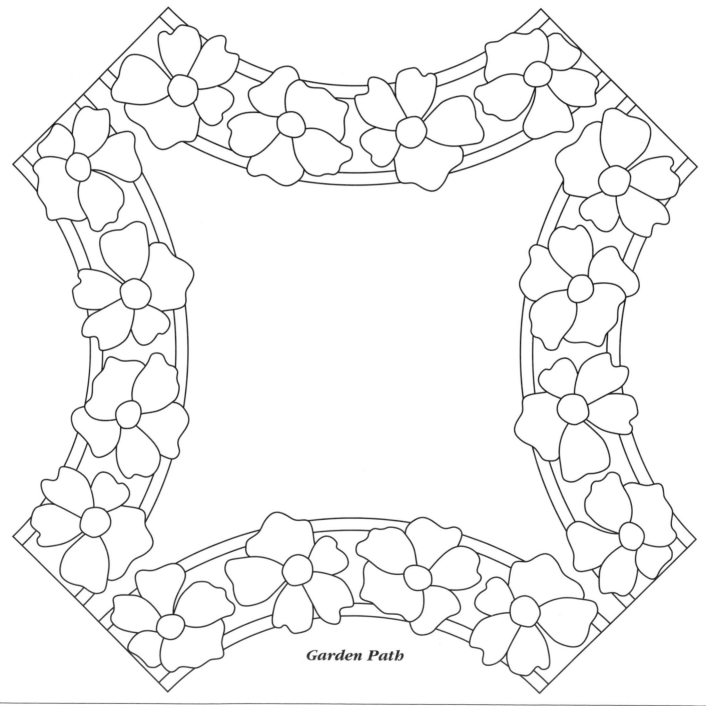

Garden Path

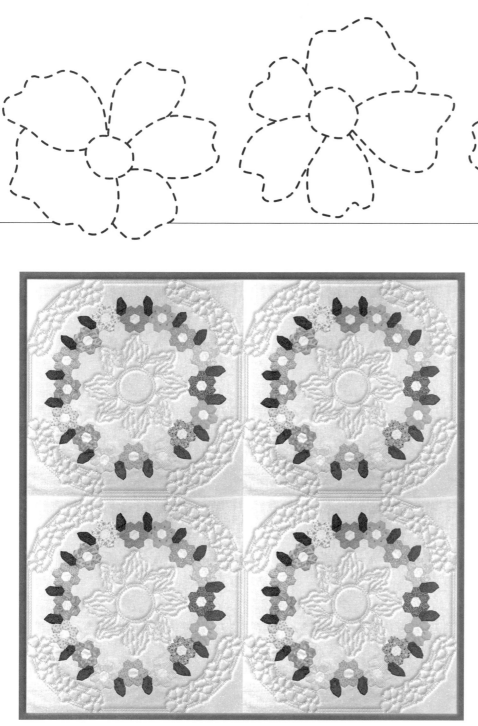

Grandmother's Floral Wreath by Caryl Johnson, West Lafayette, Indiana.

☐ Place the four quarter segments of *Windblown Garden* facing in toward the center to create a new design named *Garden Path*. Set on point.

☐ Enlarge the pattern to fit the corners of the blocks.

☐ Extend parallel lines from the rings to connect to the next repeat, as shown in Caryl Johnson's quilt above.

☐ Outline quilt around the hexagon flowers and leaves appliquéd in each block.

☐ Add the *Windblown* leaves to the center for a theme quilting motif.

**PULL-OUT
PATTERN
4" BORDER**

Identify the Design Elements

Corner

Filler

Two repeats

☐ Determine the size of the area to be quilted.

☐ Enlarge or reduce the **width** of the pattern(s) or the height of rows to fit the project.

☐ Connect the corner and enough filler pieces to extend the **length** as needed.

☐ Rotate the pattern clockwise to turn corners. Refer to illustration on opposite page.

Adapted and redesigned, from a design sent to me by Mary V. Wemhoff, Platte Center, Nebraska. Used with permission.

Connect here ▶

***Mary's
Meandering Leaves,
3½" Corner &
Border***

Helen's Hints:
Design the quilting pattern to fit one-quarter of the quilt plus **two inches**. This overlapping margin shows you if the pattern rotates, reverses, is mitered, or if any extra elements need to be repeated around the quilt.

2"

2"

Placement Diagram

☐ Notice how straight lines and flowing curves were combined in each leaf to make an outstanding pattern. This is a true element of a good design.

☐ A continuous-line pattern can be *quilted* faster by hand, sewing machine, or a long-arm quilting machine. It still needs to be *planned* first!

◄ *Connect here*

PULL-OUT PATTERN 12" BLOCK

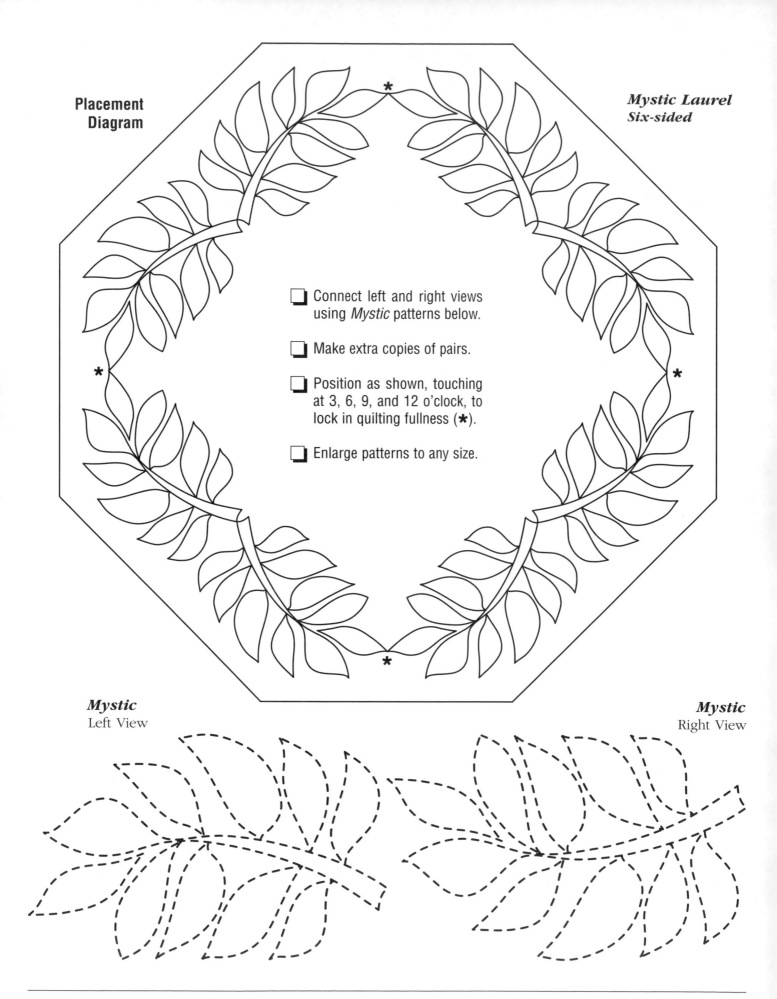

Placement Diagram

Mystic Laurel *Six-sided*

☐ Connect left and right views using *Mystic* patterns below.

☐ Make extra copies of pairs.

☐ Position as shown, touching at 3, 6, 9, and 12 o'clock, to lock in quilting fullness (✱).

☐ Enlarge patterns to any size.

Mystic Left View

Mystic Right View

Altering the Design's Shape

- [ ] Use the tip (the top five leaves) of *Mystic* to create a shortened, tightened version.

- [ ] Stretch and position leaves to emphasize a squared-off shape.

- [ ] Redraw and make extra copies.

- [ ] Pivot and connect as shown in illustration.

- [ ] This new design is named *Molen*, Dutch for windmill.

- [ ] Enlarge to any size as needed.

Mystic Molen
Set Square

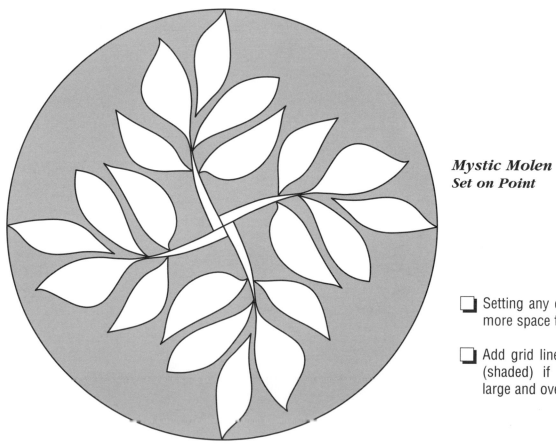

Mystic Molen
Set on Point

- [ ] Setting any design on point requires more space than using it set square.

- [ ] Add grid lines to flatten background (shaded) if the area becomes too large and overpowers the design.

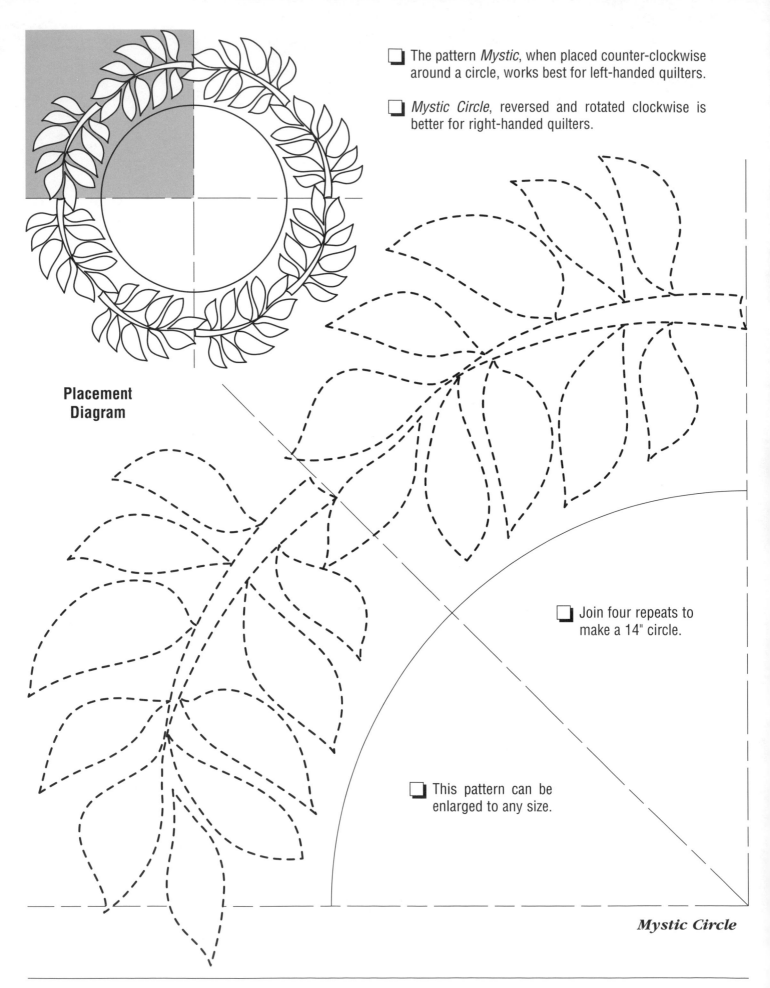

Placement Diagram

☐ The pattern *Mystic*, when placed counter-clockwise around a circle, works best for left-handed quilters.

☐ *Mystic Circle*, reversed and rotated clockwise is better for right-handed quilters.

☐ Join four repeats to make a 14" circle.

☐ This pattern can be enlarged to any size.

Mystic Circle

As seen in
American Quilter magazine,
Winter 1998.

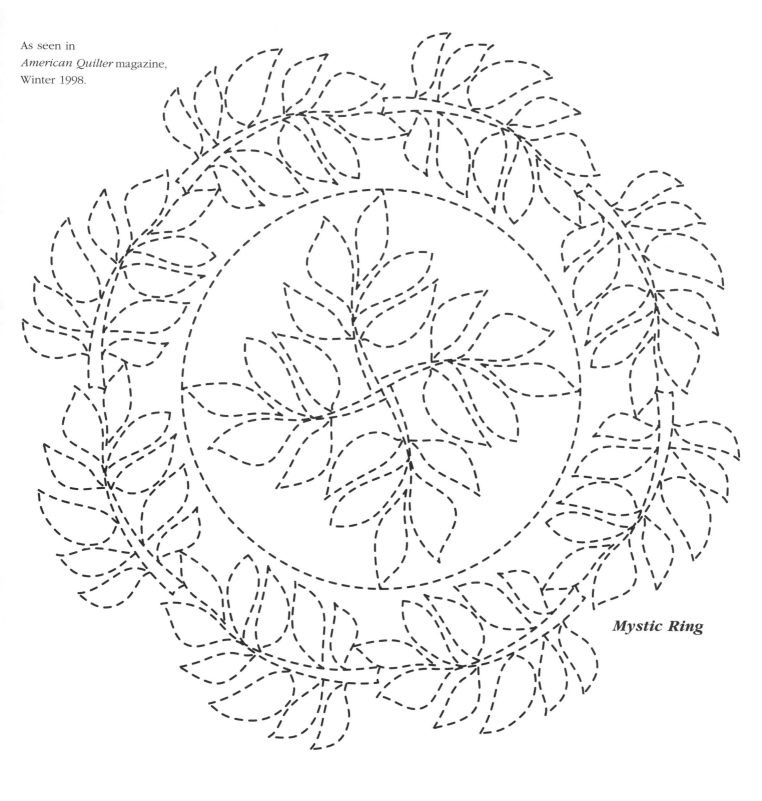

Mystic Ring

- [ ] Make eight copies of *Mystic* using the right view.
- [ ] Rotate to form a circular design, as in *Mystic Circle*.
- [ ] Enlarge to fit the area to be quilted.
- [ ] Add an inner circle ¼" away from the design.

- [ ] Use the modified version, *Mystic Molen,* for center.
- [ ] Pivot to set on point (refer to page 45).
- [ ] Reduce or enlarge to fit inside; tips touching circle.
- [ ] Rename this new combination *Mystic Ring.*

Placement Diagram

- [ ] A mirror image is formed when the pattern *Mystic* is vertically cut in half.

- [ ] Extra copies are positioned in the corner of a square, just touching (✱).

- [ ] A background grid of mitered, diagonal lines completes this new design called *Mystic Maze*.

- [ ] Two blocks, set together, are shown in the illustration above. Add more repeats for whitework quilts.

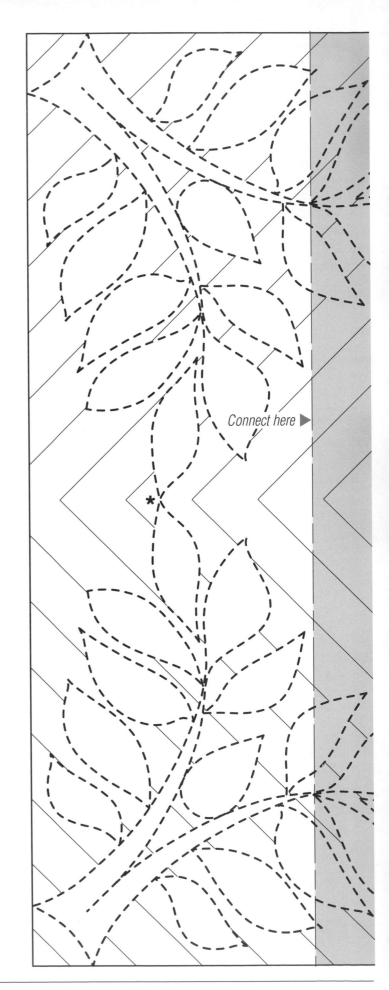

Connect here ▶

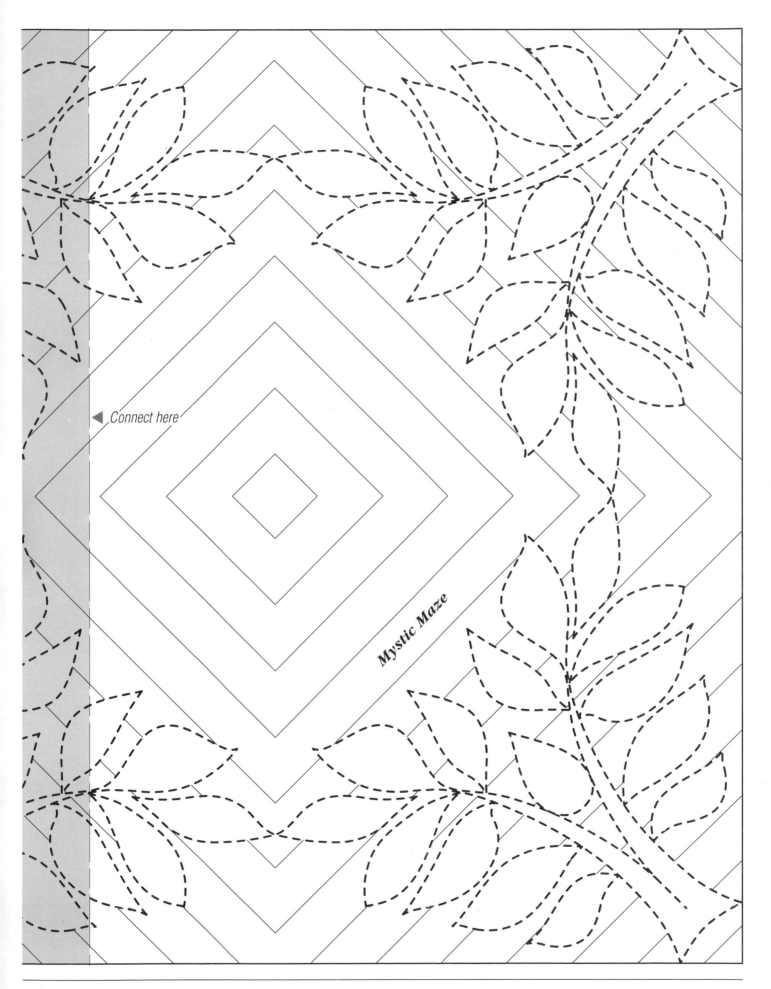

◄ *Connect here*

Mystic Maze

Chapter Four

Silhouette Stencils

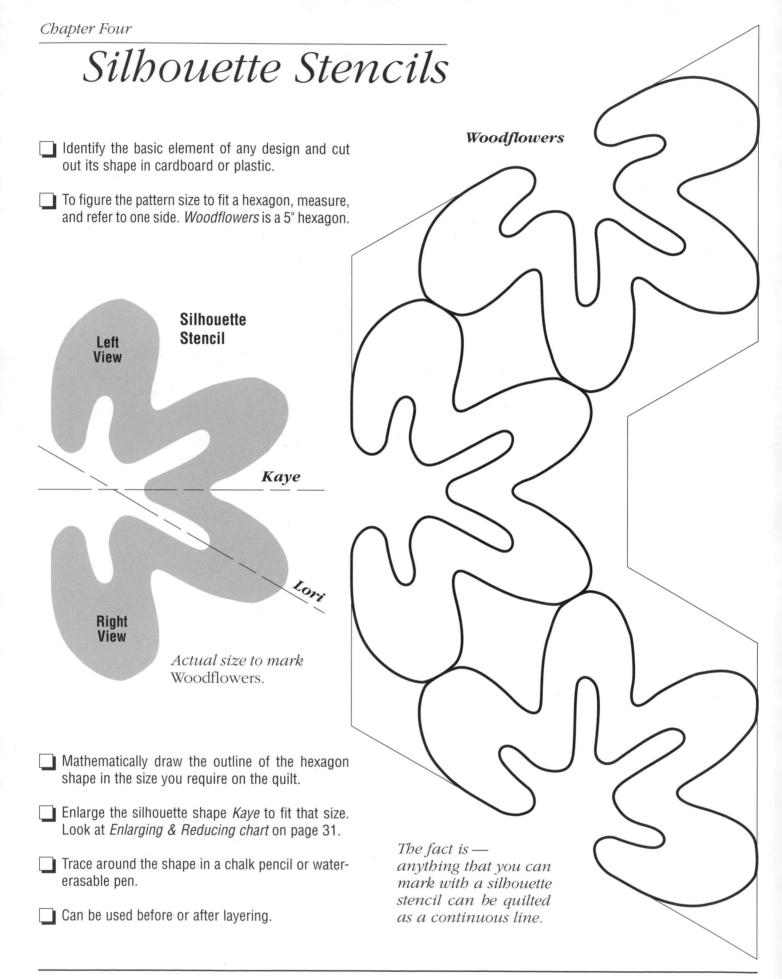

Woodflowers

☐ Identify the basic element of any design and cut out its shape in cardboard or plastic.

☐ To figure the pattern size to fit a hexagon, measure, and refer to one side. *Woodflowers* is a 5" hexagon.

Silhouette Stencil

Left View

Kaye

Lori

Right View

Actual size to mark Woodflowers.

☐ Mathematically draw the outline of the hexagon shape in the size you require on the quilt.

☐ Enlarge the silhouette shape *Kaye* to fit that size. Look at *Enlarging & Reducing chart* on page 31.

☐ Trace around the shape in a chalk pencil or water-erasable pen.

☐ Can be used before or after layering.

The fact is — anything that you can mark with a silhouette stencil can be quilted as a continuous line.

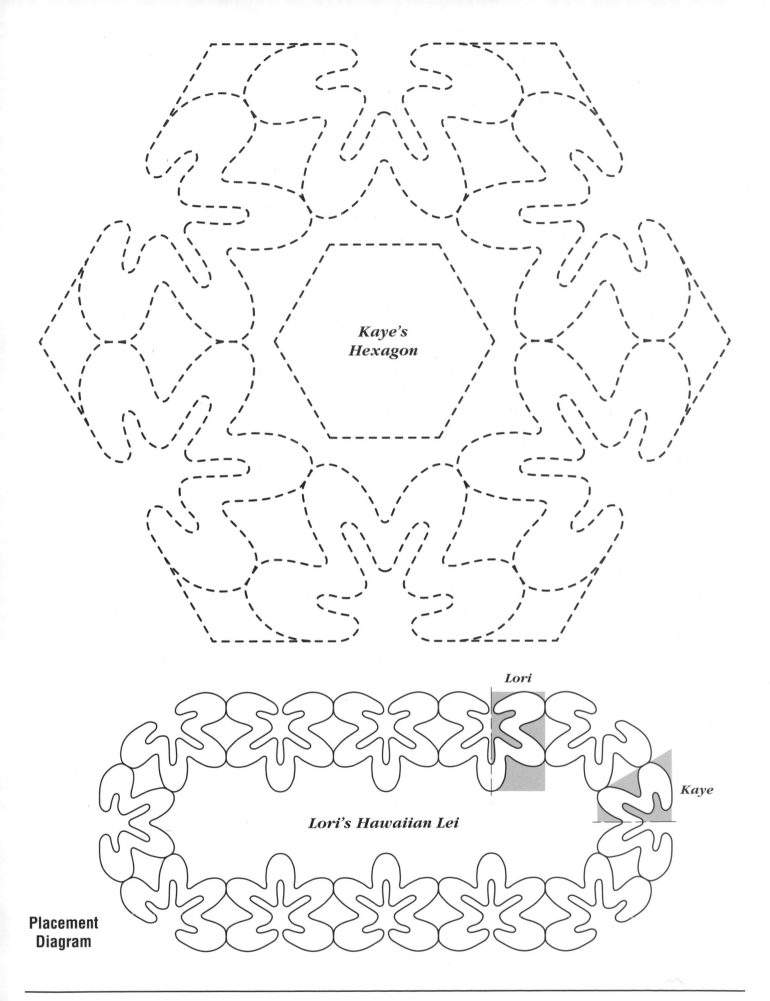

Kaye's Hexagon

Lori

Kaye

Lori's Hawaiian Lei

Placement Diagram

A Medley of Flowers

- [ ] Start collecting floral quilting designs. Adjust them all to fit 5" blocks.

- [ ] The entire *Dear Helen* series has a medley of flower and butterfly patterns. Add *Mini-Yoko* and *Mini-Star* to your collection.

- [ ] To stack three repeats, make extra copies and position flowers in line with no extra space between rows, as shown in the illustration (✻). This minimizes open areas which can distract from the overall quilting design.

- [ ] To nestle three repeats within each other, enlarge copies proportionately (see *Yoko's Flowers* on page 55). The new design formed can be used as a large center medallion pattern.

- [ ] Silhouettes can be made in any size to mark the quilt.

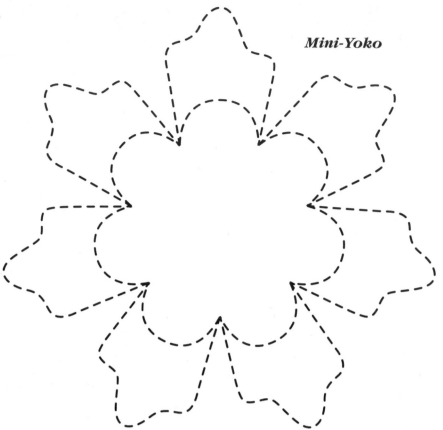

Mini-Yoko

Mini-Star

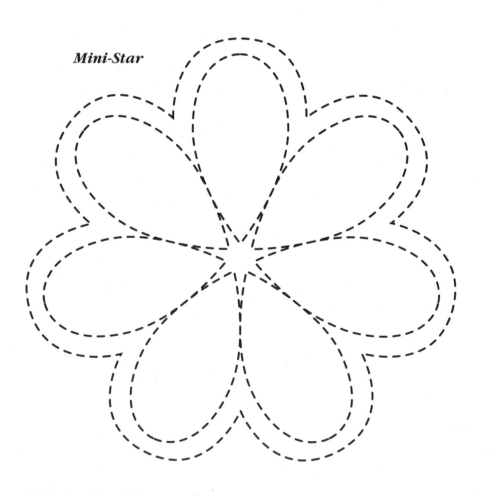

Placement Diagram

Can be quilted by hand or machine.

Star Bright

Combining Patterns

☐ Patterns can easily be enlarged or reduced to fit within each other. Refer to a proportion scale for percentages (see page 62).

☐ Start with the outside pattern, *Yoko,* and enlarge the miniature version 156%. Reduce *Mini-Star* 84%. Place inside the opening. Redraw combination, now named *Star Bright*.

☐ For the pattern shown above, the actual size silhouette stencil is provided here. Trace and cut out in cardboard or plastic. Rotate to mark.

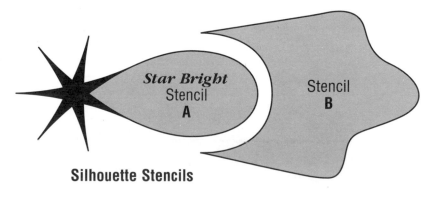

Star Bright Stencil A

Stencil B

Silhouette Stencils

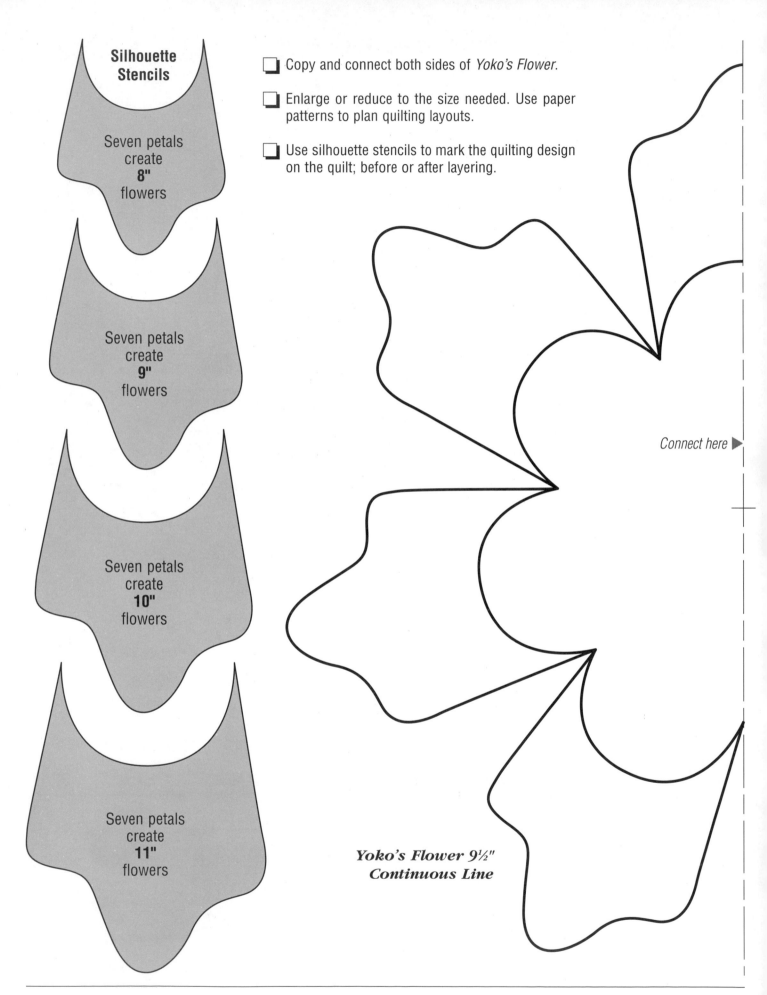

Silhouette Stencils

Seven petals
create
8"
flowers

Seven petals
create
9"
flowers

Seven petals
create
10"
flowers

Seven petals
create
11"
flowers

☐ Copy and connect both sides of *Yoko's Flower*.

☐ Enlarge or reduce to the size needed. Use paper patterns to plan quilting layouts.

☐ Use silhouette stencils to mark the quilting design on the quilt; before or after layering.

Connect here ▶

Yoko's Flower 9½"
Continuous Line

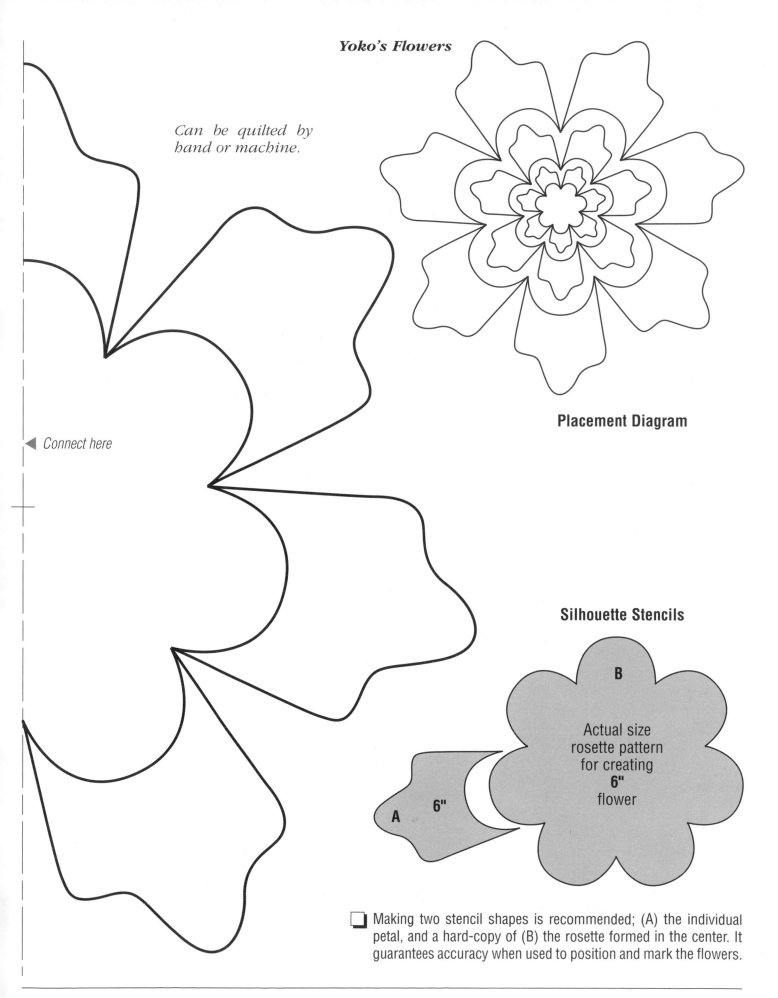

Yoko's Flowers

Can be quilted by hand or machine.

◀ *Connect here*

Placement Diagram

Silhouette Stencils

B

Actual size
rosette pattern
for creating
6"
flower

A 6"

☐ Making two stencil shapes is recommended; (A) the individual petal, and a hard-copy of (B) the rosette formed in the center. It guarantees accuracy when used to position and mark the flowers.

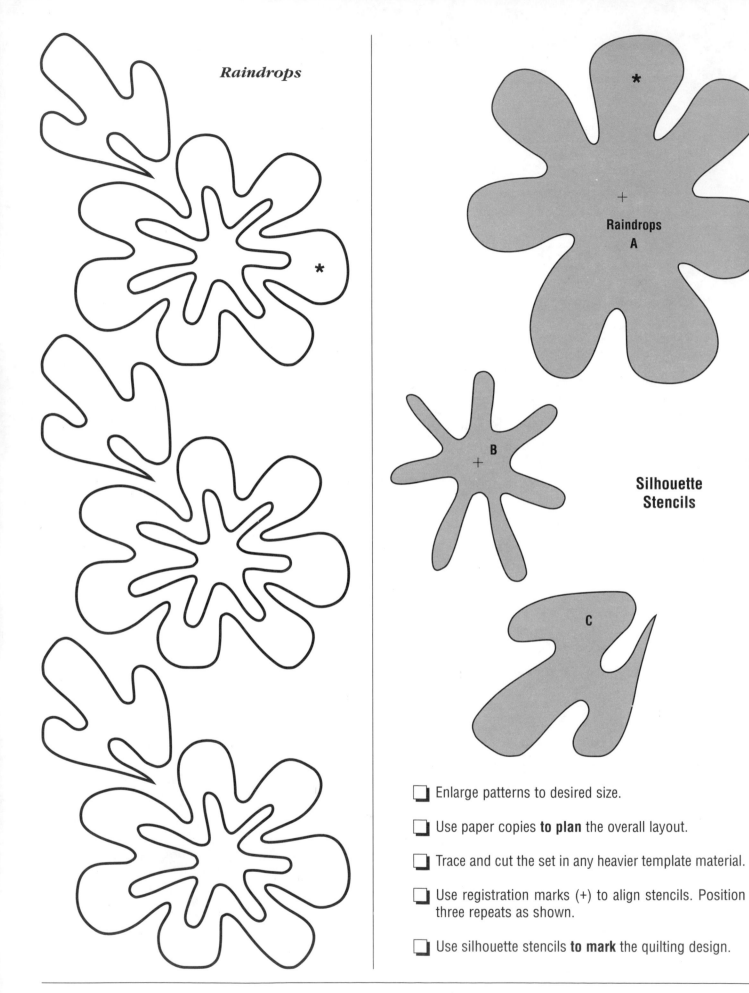

Raindrops

Raindrops A

B

Silhouette Stencils

C

C

- Enlarge patterns to desired size.

- Use paper copies **to plan** the overall layout.

- Trace and cut the set in any heavier template material.

- Use registration marks (+) to align stencils. Position three repeats as shown.

- Use silhouette stencils **to mark** the quilting design.

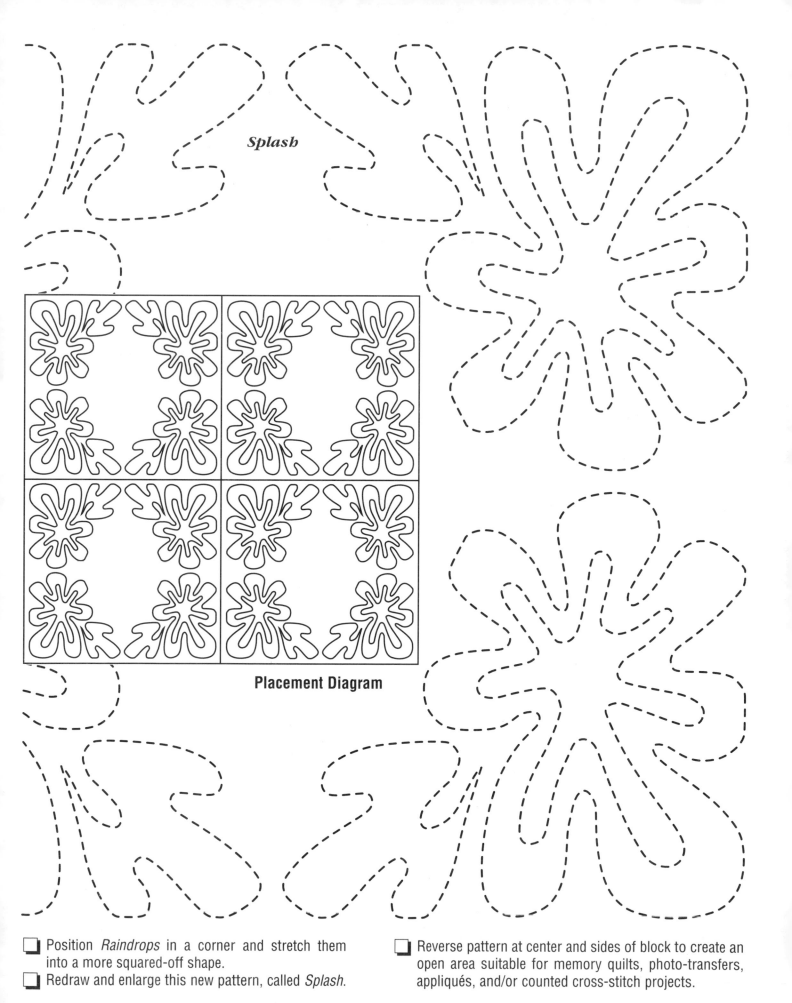

Splash

Placement Diagram

Position *Raindrops* in a corner and stretch them into a more squared-off shape.

Redraw and enlarge this new pattern, called *Splash*.

Reverse pattern at center and sides of block to create an open area suitable for memory quilts, photo-transfers, appliqués, and/or counted cross-stitch projects.

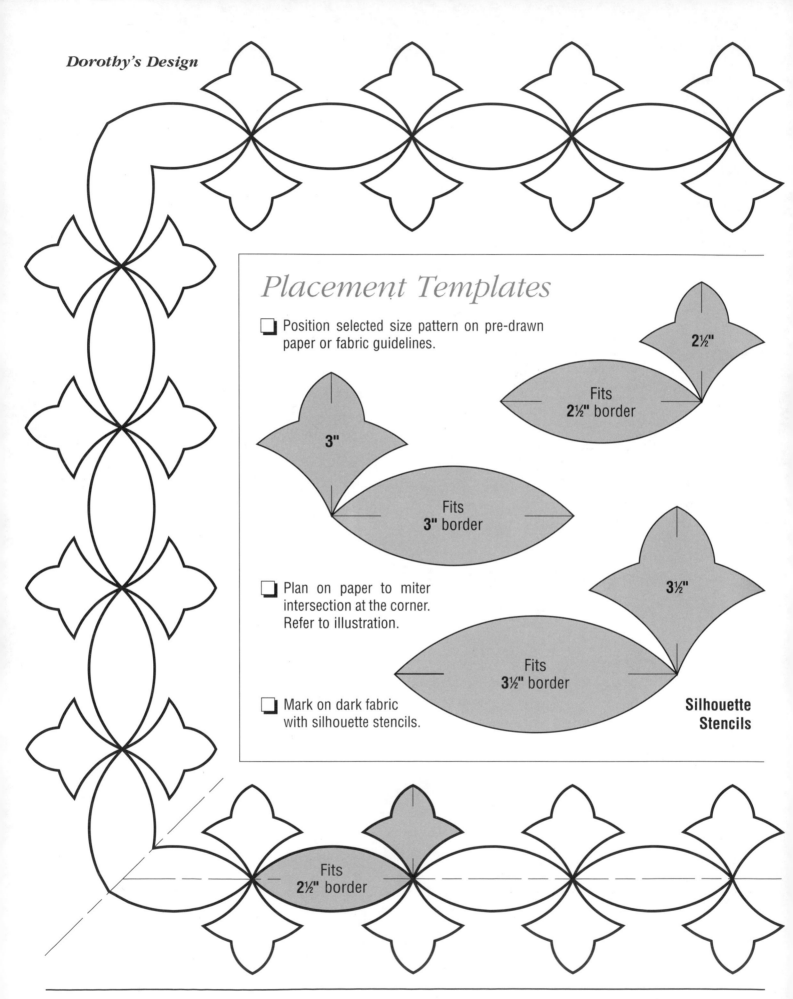

Dorothy's Design

Placement Templates

☐ Position selected size pattern on pre-drawn paper or fabric guidelines.

2½"

Fits
2½" border

3"

Fits
3" border

☐ Plan on paper to miter intersection at the corner. Refer to illustration.

3½"

Fits
3½" border

☐ Mark on dark fabric with silhouette stencils.

Silhouette Stencils

Fits
2½" border

CREATE
WITH
Helen Squire

Hand & Machine Quilting

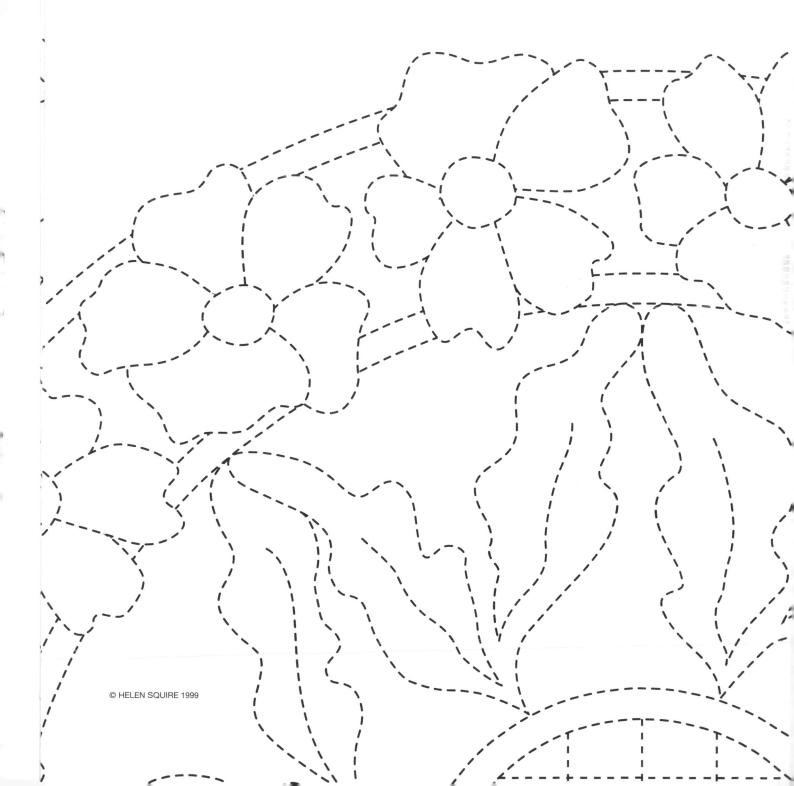

CREATE
WITH
Helen Squire

Hand & Machine Quilting

Jacob
5" Border
(page 29)

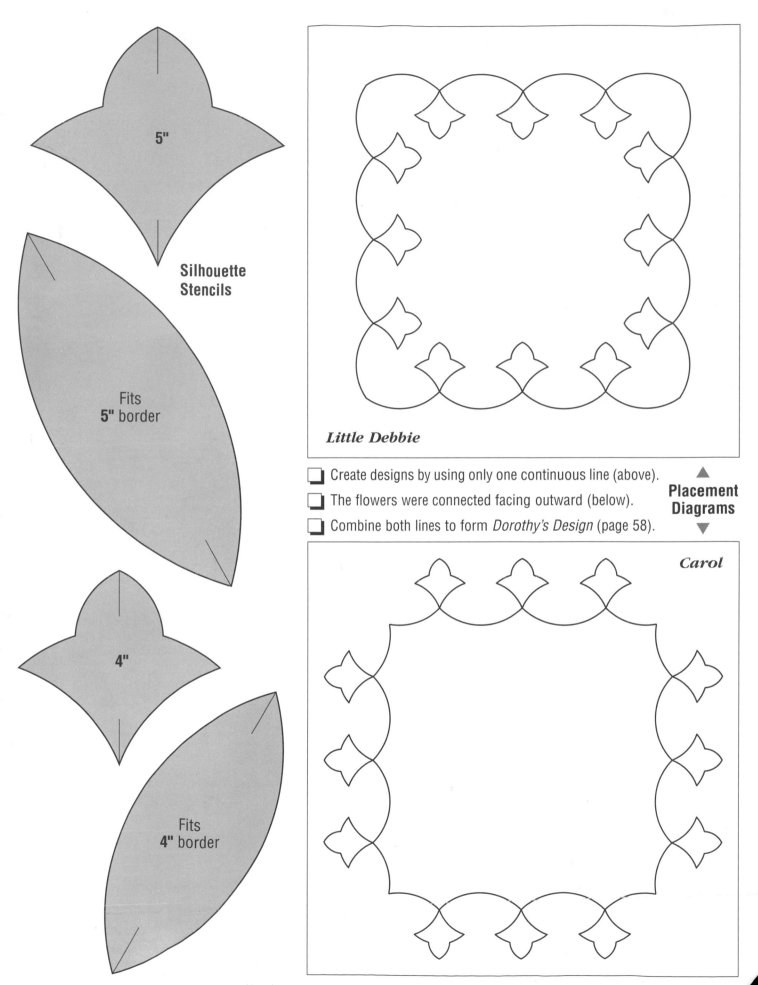

5"

Silhouette Stencils

Fits
5" border

4"

Fits
4" border

Little Debbie

☐ Create designs by using only one continuous line (above).

☐ The flowers were connected facing outward (below).

☐ Combine both lines to form *Dorothy's Design* (page 58).

▲
Placement Diagrams
▼

Carol

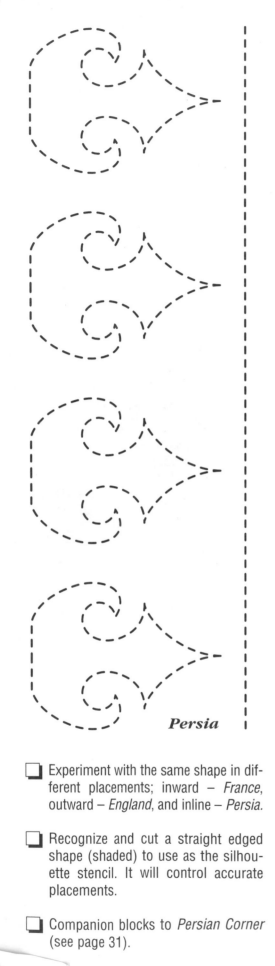

Persia

☐ Experiment with the same shape in different placements; inward – *France*, outward – *England*, and inline – *Persia*.

☐ Recognize and cut a straight edged shape (shaded) to use as the silhouette stencil. It will control accurate placements.

☐ Companion blocks to *Persian Corner* (see page 31).

Chapter Five

Grids V

Helen's Hint:

Grids have to be very accurate. Do *not* make photocopies, which can distort the grid lines.

Redraft additional sheets or sizes (use indelible ink to prevent graphite pencil smudges) and tape extra pages together for larger areas. Refer to page 35 for marking advice.

60° Hanging Diamond

½" Straight Lines

Recommended
Products & Manufacturers

STENCILS by Helen Squire

☐ **Craftco Industries, Inc.**
410 Wentworth Street North
Hamilton, Ontario L8L5W3
USA 800-661-0010
905-572-7333 / FAX 905-572-1164

☐ **Quilting Creations International, Inc.**
P.O.Box 512
Zoar, Ohio 44697
330-874-4741 / FAX 330-874-3200

☐ **The Stencil Company**
28 Castlewood Drive
Cheektowaga, New York 14227
716-656-9430 / FAX 716-668-2488

LONG-ARM QUILTING DESIGNS

☐ **Design-A-Quilt®**
95 Chestnut Street
Murray, Kentucky 42071
800-346-8227 / FAX 502-753-3007

PROPORTIONAL SCALE

☐ **Golden Threads, LLC™**
2 S 373 Seneca Drive
Wheaton, Illinois 60187
630-510-2067 / FAX 630-510-0491

LONG RULERS

☐ **The Original True Angle™**
Quint Measuring Systems
P.O.Box 280
San Ramon, California 94583-0280
800-745-5045 / 925-648-1418

*Write for their catalogs or
for the name of a retail shop near you.*

Grids